# AMAZING ME!

## A BOOK OF YOUR OWN WORLD RECORDS

written by James Buckley, Jr.

**studio** BOOKS

White Plains, New York • Montréal, Québec • Bath, United Kingdom

# Parent Note
## An Amazing Note to Adults!

Welcome to *Amazing Me! for Girls* In the pages ahead you'll find hundreds of activities that will challenge children in all kinds of fun, unusual ways. The challenges span all types of important skills for children—physical, mental, creative—and sometimes, just test their courage and perseverance! But no matter how varied they are, each challenge shares the same goal: to make children feel proud and confident about themselves!

Not every challenge is well-suited for every child. So we encourage you to get involved with your children as they use this book. Help them choose those challenges that best stretch their abilities and will most make them feel proud. With so many challenges to choose from, you're certain to find positive activities to keep any child busy for many months ahead!

A note about safety: If you ask someone to set a personal record, it's natural that they will push themselves hard. And that can create safety risks, no matter how simple the challenge. *Amazing Me!* books include a warning to children to ALWAYS be safe. As an adult, we ask that you supervise your child and reinforce this message, over and over! These challenges are first and foremost about fun. By keeping the focus there, we are certain that every single challenge will be a positive, laugh-filled experience!

Amazingly yours,

The Editors

# Table of Contents

# BE AMAZING!
## How amazing are you?
## This book gives you the chance to find out!

One way to show how amazing you are is to set world records...lots of them! Around the world, people try to gain fame and break barriers by setting world records. It's not just "how fast can you run 100 meters," but everything under the sun. There are world records in thousands of categories, from collecting pens to making giant balls of string to standing on your head.

Now it's time for you to join the ranks...with this book full of challenges designed to prove how uniquely awesome you are! How fast can you write the entire alphabet...upside down? How many braids can you make in your hair? How many times can you skip rope while hopping on one foot? You might be surprised!

So fill in the blanks...do your best...and you'll be the proud holder of dozens of world records—until you break them yourself!

## Safety First!

*You can't set personal records if you don't try hard. But far more important than setting a record is being safe and having fun. So be sensible! Make sure your parents know what you are doing and ask for their help. Be smart, have fun, and don't do ANYTHING that will put you at risk of injury, or that can cause damage. Don't do anything you or your parents are not comfortable with. Remember—fun and laughs are the real goal!*

# Measuring Success

Records have to be measured. You need to end up with a result. In this book, you'll measure a lot of different things. Here are some things you might want to keep handy:

- a stopwatch or a watch with a second hand (many phones have stopwatches on them, too)
- a measuring tape
- a scale for measuring weights
- your fingers (great for helping to count things!)
- a notebook to keep track of things that don't fit in here!
- a friend or two!

## Measuring Strings

To measure long distances, here's a cool trick. Get a ball of thick string. Using a yardstick or measuring tape, measure a foot of the string and make a mark on it. Then, along the string's length, keep measuring feet and making marks. You can then use that marked-up string as a way to measure enormously long distances!

# Fun in Five

(seconds)

For each of these challenges, you get only five seconds! Start counting now: One-Mississippi, two-Mississippi, three-Mississippi... or get a friend to help you count!

## In a Snap!*

How many times can you snap your fingers in five seconds? Now try it with your other hand!

**First Attempt:** _____

**My Amazing World Record:** _____

## Fast Lashes

You'll need someone's help to count this one: How many times can you wink in five seconds?

**First Attempt:** _____

**My Amazing World Record:** _____

How much does your count change when you wink with just your left eye, with just your right eye, and switching back and forth between the two?

## 99, 98, 97 96, 95 94, 93, 92

## Count Down

Count backward from 100 out loud. How far did you get in five seconds?

**First Attempt:** _____

**My Amazing World Record:** _____

# Kan You Kangaroo?*

How many times can you hop up and down in five seconds? (Both feet: Don't cheat!)

**First Attempt:** _____

**My Amazing
World Record:** _____

# Pucker Up!*

Loosen up those lips! How many times can you kiss your hand in five seconds?

**First Attempt:** _____

**My Amazing
World Record:** _____

# Thumbelina Would Win*

Get a clickable ball-point pen. How many times can you click it in and out in five seconds?

**First Attempt:** _____

**My Amazing
World Record:** _____

## Amazing Fact

*The average American will live more than two billion seconds. If you live to be 100 (good luck!), how many seconds will that be?*

# Hot Seat

How many times can you sit down and stand up in the same chair in five seconds?

**First Attempt:** _____

**My Amazing
World Record:** _____

(ANSWER: 3,153,600,000)

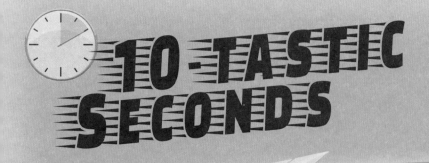

# 10-TASTIC SECONDS

Many big events start after a 10-second countdown (10! 9! 8…). These challenges are over and done in that amount of time. Take a deep breath and…stop!

## Flying Feat!*

In 10 seconds, make the best paper airplane you can. How far can it fly? Record your best distance.

**First Attempt:** _____

**My Amazing World Record:** _____

## Tennis Toss

You'll need a bunch of tennis balls for this: Put a bucket 10 feet away and see how many balls you can toss into the bucket in 10 seconds. Then move it 15 feet and try again!

**First Attempt:** _____

**My Amazing World Record:** _____

## Amazing Fact

*In 2013, Julia Piecher of Germany ran 100 meters in 14.53 seconds. Pretty good, right? Oh, did we mention she did it in high heels?*

## You Go, Girls!*

In 1988, Florence Griffith-Joyner set the 100-meter world record in 10.49 seconds. How far can you run in 10 seconds? Or else, find a football field and see what your best time is for running the whole length.

**First Attempt:** _____

**My Amazing World Record:** _____

# Fast Talker

How high can you count out loud in 10 seconds using only odd numbers?

**First Attempt:** _____

**My Amazing
World Record:** _____

How high can you count using only even numbers?

**First Attempt:** _____

**My Amazing
World Record:** _____

# Jumping Jills!

How many jumping "jills" can you do in 10 seconds? Make sure to clap at the top of each jump!

**First Attempt:** _____

**My Amazing
World Record:** _____

**Super challenge:** How many cartwheels can you do in 10 seconds?

**First Attempt:** _____

**My Amazing
World Record:** _____

# 20-second sprints

What is 20 seconds? It's one-third of a minute, or about five-thousands of an hour. Bet you don't think you can get much done in that amount of time. We bet you can!

## Super Sock-a-Thon

How many socks can you put on one foot in 20 seconds?

**First Attempt:** _____

**My Amazing
World Record:** _____

★ **Record
to Beat!** ★

**The Guinness
World Record for
the most socks
worn on one
foot is 152!**

## Quarter Turns

How many quarters can you keep spinning like tops in 20 seconds? They must stay spinning to count.

**First Attempt:** _____

**My Amazing
World Record:** _____

## Tongue-Tied

In 20 seconds, how many times can you say, "Silly Sally slurps soda slowly"?

**First Attempt:** _____

**My Amazing
World Record:** _____

# Beauty Queen in Training

Balance a book on your head. How far can you walk in 20 seconds without the book falling off (no hands allowed)?

**First Attempt:** _____

**My Amazing
World Record:** _____

Too easy? Try this challenge with two books, then three books!

**First Attempt:** _____

**My Amazing
World Record:** _____

# Set a Record
# While You Work!

See if you can whistle nonstop for 20 seconds...all in one breath! How many tries did it take you to do it?

**First Attempt:** _____

**My Amazing
World Record:** _____

# Speed Dresser

Put together a nice outfit of shirt, pants, socks, and sweater or jacket. Now, can you put all of them on in 20 seconds? See, you can get ready for school quickly!

**First Attempt:** _____

**My Amazing
World Record:** _____

# Be Fabulous in 45

In a minute, we'll get to what you can do in a minute. But first, let's go for something a little shorter: 45 seconds. Get your stopwatch and set these records!

## Penny Piles

How many pennies can you stack in 45 seconds…while blindfolded?

**First Attempt:** _____

**My Amazing World Record:** _____

## Makeup Organizer

Get all the jars and bottles of nail polish that you have (or that you can borrow). Now, in 45 seconds, can you put them all in alphabetical order of their colors?

**First Attempt:** _____

**My Amazing World Record:** _____

# Top 40 (or More!*)

How many recording artists (single or group) can you write down in 45 seconds? No repeats! Challenge your friends to top your record!

**First Attempt:** _____

**My Amazing
World Record:** _____

# Just Jumping*

How many times can you jump rope in 45 seconds? If you trip on the rope, start your count again.

**First Attempt:** _____

**My Amazing
World Record:** _____

★ **Record
to Beat!** ★

In 2006, 292 engineering students in Pune, India, successfully jumped rope simultaneously on the same rope, setting a Guinness World Record.

# Got a Minute?

A minute has 60 seconds. You will need every single one to succeed with these challenges. For these, it just takes a minute...to win it!

Mississippi

## Be Pen-Tastic!

How many times in 60 seconds can you write the word "Mississippi"?

**First Attempt:** _____

**My Amazing World Record:** _____

To give your mouth a workout, too, see how many times you can say it in a minute!

**First Attempt:** _____

**My Amazing World Record:** _____

## 52-Card Shuffle

Take a deck of cards, dump them onto the floor faceup and spread them around. In 60 seconds, how many can you put back in order? (Remember to start with all the aces, then all the 2s, 3s, 4s...)

**First Attempt:** _____

**My Amazing World Record:** _____

# Ears to You

Gather up 20 pairs of earrings. Then mix them up in a bowl. Can you make the 20 pairs again in under a minute? You'll need fast fingers! What was your time?

**First Attempt:** _____

**My Amazing
World Record:** _____

# 1-2-3-4-5...Whew!

How many of these 卌 can you write in one minute? Count the groups of five, not the individual lines.

**First Attempt:** _____

**My Amazing
World Record:** _____

# As Easy as Z-Y-X!

Can you recite the alphabet backward in 60 seconds? Try doing it without looking at the letters!

**First Attempt:** _____

**My Amazing
World Record:** _____

## Amazing Fact

*Soldiers in the American Revolution were known as "minutemen." It was said they could dress to be ready to join a battle...in just a minute!*

Z Y X W V U T S R Q P O N
M L K J I H G F E D C B A

# 5-Minute Marathons

After doing things in 5, 10, or 20 seconds, the challenges on this page will seem like they take a *realllly* long time! But sometimes the hardest things take the most time! Are you up to these endurance challenges?

## All Fall Down

How many dominoes can you stand up in a row in five minutes? When your time is up, send them toppling! Only the dominoes that fell count toward your record!

**First Attempt:** _____

**My Amazing
World Record:** _____

## Fill 'er Up

You need a bowl filled with water, a large drinking glass and a tablespoon. Put the glass at least 20 feet away from the bowl. How much of the glass can you fill in five minutes with water from the bowl, using only the spoon?

**First Attempt:** _____

**My Amazing
World Record:** _____

# A Real Run-On

Get a pencil and paper. Ready? Now write the longest sentence you can in five minutes. The sentence has to make sense (mostly!). Use lots of commas and dashes to keep it going. Measure how you did by counting the words.

**First Attempt:** _____

**My Amazing
World Record:** _____

# A Running Read-On

Prefer reading to writing? Get a favorite book. How much of it can you read out loud in five minutes? Measure by counting how many book lines you read. Remember to breathe!

**First Attempt:** _____

**My Amazing
World Record:** _____

## Amazing Fact

*A company in the Netherlands tops itself every year. Weijers Domino Productions regularly puts up displays of more than four million dominoes…and then knocks them over!*

# Pasta Pastime

For this one, grab a piece of raw spaghetti and a bunch of raw penne pasta pieces. Scatter the penne around the edges of a table. Put one end of the spaghetti in your mouth and use the other end to pick up pieces of penne and put them into a bowl. How many did you place in the bowl in five minutes?

**First Attempt:** _____

**My Amazing
World Record:** _____

# STICK WITH IT!

Many world records are set for endurance—people doing the same thing for a *lonnnng* time. For each of these challenges see how long you can do it...and then see if you can do better the next time! (Some of these could take days...)

## Hang in There

Remember, for these challenges, there is no time limit. In fact, the longer the better! Record how long you can...

| | **First Attempt** | **My Amazing World Record** |
|---|---|---|
| Stare without blinking | _____ | _____ |
| Stand on one foot | _____ | _____ |
| Hold a push-up position | _____ | _____ |
| Hold an orange straight out in front of you | _____ | _____ |
| Balance a balloon on your head | _____ | _____ |
| Hold your breath | _____ | _____ |
| Bounce a ball | _____ | _____ |
| Maintain a big smile | _____ | _____ |
| Keep your room clean | _____ | _____ |

*(Nah, just kidding...no one can do that for long!)*

# Flying Feathers!

For this challenge, you need a feather. Pick one that's fluffy and light, not stiff with a hard point. Now see how long you can keep it floating above your head using only your breath to keep it up there. Huff and puff and don't let it fall!

**First Attempt:** _____

**My Amazing
World Record:** _____

# Super Endurance Challenges!

Record how long you can…

| | First Attempt | My Amazing World Record |
|---|---|---|
| Do everything with your opposite hand | _____ | _____ |
| Go without using the word "like" | _____ | _____ |
| Wear a shirt backward before someone notices | _____ | _____ |
| Not eat any candy | _____ | _____ |
| Not wear the color blue | _____ | _____ |
| Walk backward everywhere | _____ | _____ |
| Start every sentence with "Yo,…" | _____ | _____ |
| Speak with an English accent | _____ | _____ |

*(If you're English, try speaking with a French accent!)*

# Play with Paper

Paper performers: Please procure pieces of paper…and patience. And perhaps a pen. (P.S.: Plain notebook paper will work perfectly.)

## Line 'em Up!

How many times can you write your name on a piece of paper that is 5 x 7 inches? None of the names can touch or cross.

**First Attempt:** _____

**My Amazing
World Record:** _____

## Super Snowflake

Remember how to make a paper snowflake out of a folded sheet of paper? Good! What is the most cuts you can make and still have a snowflake that holds together?

**First Attempt:** _____

**My Amazing
World Record:** _____

# Delicately, Please!*

Use some recycled paper for this one: What is the narrowest strip of paper you can rip from a bigger piece?

**First Attempt:** _____

**My Amazing
World Record:** _____

# Hats On!*

Do you know how to make a hat out of newspaper? It's a pretty cool trick. Ask your mom or dad to show you or look on the Internet. How fast you can you fold one of your own?

**First Attempt:** _____

**My Amazing
World Record:** _____

# Bonus Challenge:

How long can you make a sentence in which ALL the words start with the same letter? It must make sense!

**First Attempt:** _____

**My Amazing
World Record:** _____

# Supply Closet

Your teacher gives you a list of stuff you need for school. You need that stuff to do your work and be creative. But that doesn't mean you can't have fun with it, too! Dig into your school supplies for the materials you need to master these challenges.

## Another Kind of Makeup

How many sticky notes can you stick to your face in 30 seconds? Only count those that are still on your face at the 30-second mark!

**First Attempt:** _____

**My Amazing World Record:** _____

**Super Challenge:** How many can you stick on your body with no time limit? They have to stay stuck to count!

**First Attempt:** _____

**My Amazing World Record:** _____

## Finger Ringer

How many rubber bands can get onto one finger? Here's the trick: you have to use that finger to get them on. (Hint: Make a pile of rubber bands before you start.)

**First Attempt:** _____

**My Amazing World Record:** _____

# No. 2 Art

How fast can you spell "pencil"? Wait—there's a trick. You have to place actual pencils end to end to form the shapes of each letter on a table, one letter at a time! You'll need at least 16 pencils to spell the word!

**First Attempt:** _____

**My Amazing World Record:** _____

## Amazing Fact

*Many pencils are colored yellow. Here's why: The first good pencils came from China. To show that their pencils were of Chinese quality, makers painted them yellow. In China, yellow means royalty or…the best!*

# Connect the Clips

What's the longest paper-clip chain you can make in 30 seconds? Measure by inches, not by how many clips.

**First Attempt:** _____

**My Amazing World Record:** _____

# Your Name in Metal

Test your stapling abilities! How fast can you use a stapler to build letters that spell your name?

**First Attempt:** _____

**My Amazing World Record:** _____

# FUN WITH TOYS

You'll need to gather some props to set these records. So now...record setters: to the toy closet!

## Sky High!

What is the tallest single-brick Lego tower you can build?

**First Attempt:** _____

**My Amazing World Record:** _____

Then try for the longest wall you can build that is two bricks high.

**First Attempt:** _____

**My Amazing World Record:** _____

## Chew for the Gold

Got some bubble gum? See how many bubbles you can blow and pop in 30 seconds.

**First Attempt:** _____

**My Amazing World Record:** _____

## Stuffed with Friends

How many stuffed animals can you stuff inside your shirt? How many more can you fit if someone helps?

**First Attempt:** _____

**My Amazing World Record:** _____

# Mega-Bounce

You need a small super-bouncy ball and a mug.
Set the mug against a wall. Stand six feet away and
bounce the ball into the mug. How many tries does
it take to get the ball in?

**First Attempt:** _____

**My Amazing
World Record:** _____

**Super Challenge:** Use three balls and three mugs.
How many tries does it take to get one ball in each mug?

**First Attempt:** _____

**My Amazing
World Record:** _____

# Dress-Up Dare

You'll need a doll and at least five dresses for
the doll. In 60 seconds, how many times can
you dress and undress the doll completely?
Can you get through all five dresses?

## Amazing Fact

*In 2012, a group of
students in Maryland
collected more than
5,300 stuffed animals!
They donated them all
to local charities and
to orphanages in
other countries.*

**First Attempt:** _____

**My Amazing
World Record:** _____

# Time to Talk

Talking is one of your favorite things to do, right? And who doesn't love to sing? Now use your voice to help you set some personal records!

## Laaaaaaa!*

Sing out! How long can you sing one note ("Laaaa" works well) without taking a breath? Don't worry if you're in tune or not!

**First Attempt:** _____

**My Amazing
World Record:** _____

## Opera Time!*

Stand next to a piano (though not one at a store; you might frighten the customers). Sing the lowest note you possibly can, and find that note on the piano. Then sing the highest note you can, and find it on the piano. How many white keys are in between your lowest and highest notes?

**First Attempt:** _____

**My Amazing
World Record:** _____

# Chatty Cathy

How chatty are you? Let's find out! How many times can you say "Chatty Cathy" before getting tongue-tied? Practice makes perfect!

**First Attempt:** _____

**My Amazing World Record:** _____

# Way to Whistle!

How many times can you whistle the tune "Mary Had a Little Lamb" in 20 seconds? How many times can you sing the song?

**First Attempt:** _____

**My Amazing World Record:** _____

# Help Yourself

For these challenges, your personal world record gets a bit more personal. Time to use your body to set a record or two!

## In a Pinch!

How many clothespins can you attach to one ear at one time? You can attach clothespins to other clothespins to do this challenge!

**First Attempt:** _____

**My Amazing
World Record:** _____

## Tough to Tie

While barefoot, have a friend tie your hands together with a scarf or a sock. Now see how fast you can pull on your socks and then pull on and tie your sneakers!

**First Attempt:** _____

**My Amazing
World Record:** _____

## A Tale of Two Tails

You need a friend that has hair long enough to braid. How many braids can you make in your friend's hair? How many can you make in your own hair?

**First Attempt:** _____

**My Amazing
World Record:** _____

# Tattoo You!

How many temporary tattoos can you apply to one of your arms? They can't overlap!

**First Attempt:** _____

**My Amazing
World Record:** _____

# Hat Rack

How many hats can you wear on your head at one time? If the stack gets too high for you to reach, you can ask a friend to help.

**First Attempt:** _____

**My Amazing
World Record:** _____

# Fingernail Fury

How fast can you put one coat of nail polish on all ten fingers? Add one second to your time whenever you get paint on your fingers instead of your nails!

**First Attempt:** _____

**My Amazing
World Record:** _____

## Amazing Fact

*The first people to use nail polish were the ancient Chinese, more than 5,000 years ago. The royal classes used silver and gold colors to show off how important they were!*

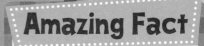

# WRITE ON!

Test your writing and drawing abilities with these artistic challenges. Don't worry; you won't be graded! No art expertise needed!

## Tiny Shapes

How fast can you draw all these shapes onto one sticky note, using your non-writing hand? The shapes are a square, rectangle, octagon, circle, oval, diamond, heart, pentagon, and triangle.

**First Attempt:** _____

**My Amazing World Record:** _____

## That's My Dog!

Look at a picture of a dog (or at a real dog if you have one handy!). Now close your eyes and try to draw a picture of that dog in 60 seconds. How did you do?

# Up Is Down

How fast can you write the entire alphabet...
with each letter upside down?!

**First Attempt:** _____

**My Amazing
World Record:** _____

How about upside down AND backward?
To grade yourself, look at your work in a mirror!

**First Attempt:** _____

**My Amazing
World Record:** _____

**Super Challenge:** Now try writing backward in script! How
quickly can you write your full name in script backward (and it
must look correct in a mirror!)?

**First Attempt:** _____

**My Amazing
World Record:** _____

# Get the Point?

How long can you balance a pencil on one
finger using just the point? See if you can
do it longer using the eraser end.

**First Attempt:** _____

**My Amazing
World Record:** _____

## Amazing Fact

*Next time you're in
St. Louis, visit the City
Museum. There you
can see—but not write
with—a 76-foot-long
yellow pencil.*

# THE CHOPSTICK CHALLENGE!

Are you a super picker-upper? Prove it! Using chopsticks, how many of each of these things can you pick up in one minute? *Zhù nî háoyùn!* (That means "good luck" in Chinese.)

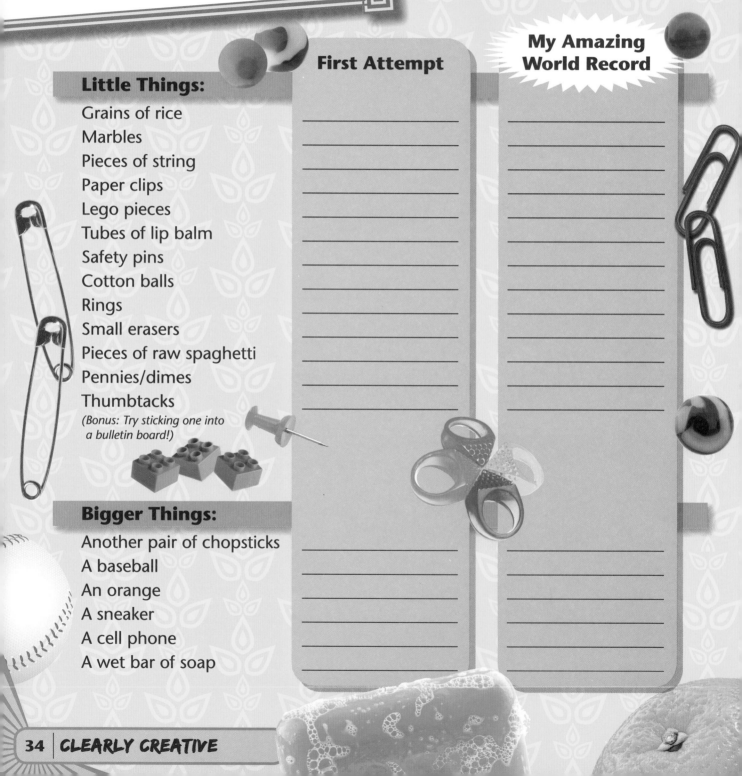

**First Attempt**

**My Amazing World Record**

## Little Things:

Grains of rice
Marbles
Pieces of string
Paper clips
Lego pieces
Tubes of lip balm
Safety pins
Cotton balls
Rings
Small erasers
Pieces of raw spaghetti
Pennies/dimes
Thumbtacks
*(Bonus: Try sticking one into a bulletin board!)*

## Bigger Things:

Another pair of chopsticks
A baseball
An orange
A sneaker
A cell phone
A wet bar of soap

# SUPER-DUPER CHALLENGE

Want to amaze your friends and family? Learn to use chopsticks with either hand. It will take lots of practice. But once you learn it, you will find many ways to impress others. Once you are a chopstick master, see how many of these things you can do using one or two sets of sticks!

❏ Put on your socks.

❏ Tie your shoe. If you can't make a bow, aim for a simple knot.

❏ Play a card game in which you must use the chopsticks to draw and discard.

❏ Read a book and use the chopsticks to hold it and turn the pages.

❏ Make your bed!

❏ Eat your breakfast, lunch, and dinner!

What other things can you think of?

_____

_____

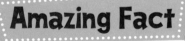

## Amazing Fact

*People in China have been using chopsticks for more than 3,000 years. By 500 A.D., chopsticks had spread to other Asian countries.*

# YOU LIKE TO MOVE IT!

These races challenge more than just your feet! It's best if one of your friends sits out to time and judge the races. Take turns being the timer!

## Animal Races!

In this race, get into a frog position and get hopping! First person to hop 15 yards is the winner! Who was the fastest frog? What was her time?

**Fastest Frog:**_____ **Time:**_____

**My Time:** _____

On a clean floor, get down on your belly, put your arms at your side, and slither like a snake! Who can cross the floor fastest without using their arms or hands?

**Swiftest Snake:** _____ **Time:**_____

**My Time:** _____

Put four on the floor and race like a greyhound! You must run on all fours—no jumping allowed! Who was top dog?

**Top Dog:** _____ **Time:**_____

**My Time:** _____

# A Classic!

The wheelbarrow race has been around for years. Find a flat space outside, measure out 50 feet, and get racing! How fast was the winning wheelbarrow?

**The Winner:** _____ **Time:** _____

**My Time:** _____

**Super Challenge:** Make the race longer! At the 50-foot marker, switch places and head back to the start. How fast was the winning team?

**Winning Team:** _____ **Time:** _____

**My Time:** _____

# Chinny-Chin-Chin

For this race, each participant needs to hold a ball under her chin while running (tennis balls and baseballs work well). First person to run 25 yards without dropping her ball wins!

**The Winner:** _____

**My Time:** _____

# Inflate-a-Thon

Grab a bag of balloons, and give three empty balloons to each friend. Blow up one balloon to use as "model balloon." Then get blowing! Which friend can blow up their three balloons to be the same size as the model the fastest?

**The Winner:** _____ **Time:** _____

**My Time:** _____

## Amazing Fact

*A man knitted a 12-foot-long scarf. No big deal, right? Well, he did it while running a marathon in Kansas City, Missouri, in 2013!*

# Jumpin' Gymnastics!

Ready for a workout? Take on these challenges and set a stack of new amazing world records!

## Over and Over and Over...

Which friend in your group can do the most somersaults in a row? Do this challenge one at a time or as a group. How many somersaults did the super somersaulter do? (Say that five times fast!)

**The Winner:** _____ **How Many:** _____

**My Amazing World Record:** _____

## Monkeying Around

Head to a playground that has monkey bars. Have each person hang from a bar for as long as she can. Who's the top banana? How long was she hanging?

**The Winner:** _____ **Time:** _____

**My Amazing World Record:** _____

# Centipede

Get at least five friends and stand very close together, all facing the same way. Each friend holds the waist of the person in front of her. Now see how many steps you can take ALL TOGETHER without tangling or tripping. Here's a hint: Make sure everyone starts on the same foot!

**The Winner:** _____ **How Many:**_____

**My Amazing World Record:** _____

★ **Record to Beat!** ★

**Ashrita Furman holds a unique world record. He has the most Guinness World Records, with more than 125. Most are crazy calisthenics like these: most forward rolls, walking in the heaviest shoes, and farthest water balloon toss!**

# High-Speed Jumping Jacks

Jumping jacks are most fun when done fast. They can also be exhausting! Gather your best friends and see who can do the most in one minute.

**The Winner:** _____ **How Many:**_____

**My Amazing World Record:** _____

# Group Plank!

Do you know the starting push-up position? Straight back, straight arms, knees off the ground. Get a big group together and see who can hold that position the longest!

**The Winner:** _____ **Time:**_____

**My Amazing World Record:** _____

# Fashion Fiesta!

Time to hit the closet for the gear you need to face these challenges. No fashion sense needed—just a sense of adventure and fun! (Though fast fingers might help, too!)

## Ready, Set, Knot!

Get three or more friends together and divide into pairs. Untie all your shoes. The challenge: See which team can tie their shoes the fastest. The trick—you are each allowed to use only one hand. But you can work together to tie each shoe!

**The Winners:** _____ **Time:** _____

**My Amazing World Record:** _____

## Shoe-be-doo-be-doo

Who can pour and drink a cup of milk the fastest? Use a plastic cup. No challenge, you say? Well, you are wearing shoes on your hands when you do it!

**First Attempt:** _____

**Our Amazing World Record:** _____

## Quick Change!

Find a T-shirt that's big enough to fit all the friends in your group. Now see how fast you can relay-wear it! What's your best time for everyone in the group to put it on and take it off in turn?

**First Attempt:** _____

**Our Amazing World Record:** _____

## A Sleeve-a-pede

This needs long-sleeved shirts and many friends. How long a line can you get of people grabbing their partners' arms inside one another's sleeves? Sort of like a human chain, but all covered in shirts!

**First Attempt:** _____

**Our Amazing
World Record:** _____

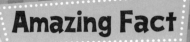

## Button-Up

You need a button-down shirt for each challenger in this one. Unbutton the shirts, blindfold each person, and then get buttoning! Who buttoned her shirt perfectly (all buttons in the correct holes) the fastest?

**The Winner:** _____ **Time:** _____

**My Amazing
World Record:** _____

**SIZE**

**XXXXL**

## Really Big Shirt

Find the most enormous T-shirt you can. Ask your local football team. Or try a "big and tall" men's store. Then see how many of your friends can get inside it all at once.

**First Attempt:** _____

**Our Amazing
World Record:** _____

# Can You Spell Awesome?

**Many brains make for some pretty awesome work! For these challenges, compete against your gal pals to see who has the fastest word-brain!**

## Hidden Words

How many words can your group make using only the letters from AMAZING ME?

**First Attempt:** _____

**Our Amazing World Record:** _____

Now use the letters from BATRACHOPHAGOUS. Bonus points if you can guess what it means.

**First Attempt:** _____

**Our Amazing World Record:** _____

What were the longest words you came up with for both challenges?

**First Attempt:** _____

**Our Amazing World Record:** _____

## Amazing Fact

*Here are some recent most-popular girls' names given to babies around the world:*

**U.S.A.:** *Sophia*
**Australia:** *Ruby*
**Canada:** *Emma*
**Japan:** *Yui*
**Poland:** *Julia*

# Super Challenge: Ready to Write?

For these challenges, the goal is to write as many words on a piece of paper as possible that fit the challenge. Put one minute on the clock for each challenge. Spelling counts! Record who wins each event!

Write as many two-letter words as you can in one minute. (Hey, we just gave you two right there! Yikes! There's another one!)

**Winner:** _____ **How Many Words:**_____

Let's make it harder…how many three-letter words can you scribble in one minute?

**Winner:** _____ **How Many Words:**_____

Now make it seven-letter words! Awesome!

**Winner:** _____ **How Many Words:**_____

How many two-syllable verbs? Go!

**Winner:** _____ **How Many Words:**_____

# Chill Jill and Sassy Kassie

How many words can you think of that rhyme with your name?

**Number of Words:** _____

Compete to see whose name is the rhymiest. Whose name had the most rhymes? You can also work together to come up with the longest list for all your names.

**Who Is Rhymiest:** _____

**My Amazing World Record:** _____

# Build It Up!

Start with any letter, then take turns adding one letter at a time. What's the longest word you can make that way? Keep trying…there are some great words out there!

**First Attempt:** _____

**Our Amazing World Record:** _____

# SUPER SCAVENGER HUNT

Break into teams of at least two people. Now, how fast can each team find the things in the lists below? Each group should take a turn while the other groups time them. Scavengers can either gather the objects or use a digital camera or phone camera to take pictures of each thing. Add 30 seconds to the search time for each object that wasn't found.

## In Your Room

| | Team 1 | Team 2 |
|---|---|---|
| Something that starts with "K" | ☐ | ☐ |
| Something that writes in a color other than blue or black | ☐ | ☐ |
| An item of clothing that's very fuzzy | ☐ | ☐ |
| Something with your picture on or in it | ☐ | ☐ |
| Five socks that do not match | ☐ | ☐ |
| A book that is at least 150 pages long | ☐ | ☐ |
| A picture of food you would eat at breakfast | ☐ | ☐ |
| Any image of an animal other than a dog or cat | ☐ | ☐ |

Total objects scavenged: _____  _____

# In Your Kitchen

| | Team 1 | Team 2 |
|---|---|---|
| A pot holder | ☐ | ☐ |
| A dish that you used when you were a baby or a toddler | ☐ | ☐ |
| A spoon big enough to hold an orange | ☐ | ☐ |
| A spice that starts with the letter "M" | ☐ | ☐ |
| A vegetable that you've never tried (that will be easy!) | ☐ | ☐ |
| Something that both cats and people eat | ☐ | ☐ |
| Four things that you use to clean up | ☐ | ☐ |
| A drinking glass with words on it | ☐ | ☐ |

Total objects scavenged: _____  _____

# In Your House

| | Team 1 | Team 2 |
|---|---|---|
| Three different colored pens | ☐ | ☐ |
| A roll of tape at least two inches across | ☐ | ☐ |
| A picture of someone whose last name starts with "D" | ☐ | ☐ |
| Each of these batteries: AA, AAA, and D | ☐ | ☐ |
| A hat that doesn't fit you | ☐ | ☐ |
| Two books you've never read but you want to | ☐ | ☐ |
| An electronic gadget that doesn't work anymore | ☐ | ☐ |
| A postcard from a foreign country | ☐ | ☐ |

Total objects scavenged: _____  _____

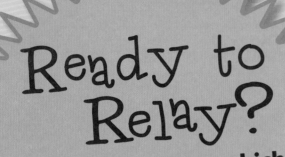

# Ready to Relay?

### Keep time to see which team sets the world record!

For each of these relays, measure and mark a course that is about 15 yards from start to finish. Split your friends into even-numbered teams. Half the racers stand at the start line and half stand at the 15-yard finish line. Each racer must do the task given, then tag the next racer, who then returns to where the first racer came from (and tags the next racer).

## Don't Eat the Game Pieces!

You need a spoon for each racer and some small candies. Each racer must run with the candy in her spoon to the next racer and transfer the candy to the next person's spoon. If the candy is dropped at any time, the racer must go back to the start!

**Winning Team:** _____ **Time:**_____

**Second Place:**_____ **Time:**_____

## Piggyback

Piggyback time: Hop on for a ride to the 15-yard mark. Then switch positions and race back. Make sure all racers pair up according to size!

**Winning Team:** _____ **Time:**_____

**Second Place:**_____ **Time:**_____

## Amazing Fact

*Each year at Valentine's Day, the Necco candy company produces more than eight billion of those little hearts with cute sayings on them.*

# Close Friends

Get up close and personal with your BFFs. For this relay, you must run with an orange under your chin. To tag your partner, you must pass the orange to her without using your hands!

**Winning Team:** _____ **Time:** _____

**Second Place:** _____ **Time:** _____

# Watch the Balloon!

Use large balloons for this relay. Each racer must keep the balloon in the air while running to the next racer. If the balloon touches the ground, go back to the start!

**Winning Team:** _____ **Time:** _____

**Second Place:** _____ **Time:** _____

# On and Off...and On

You need a hat, a big jacket, and some large shoes. The first person puts everything on and runs to the next person and takes those clothes off. The second person then puts on the same hat, jacket, and shoes. And so on...first team to have everyone dress and undress wins!

**Winning Team:** _____ **Time:** _____

**Second Place:** _____ **Time:** _____

For an extra challenge, add sweatpants. For an even bigger challenge, make the course 30 yards!

# FACE-TO-FACE

For all of these challenges, two people compete against each other. Have fun and good luck!

## Book It!

Who can make the tallest tower of stacked books in 30 seconds? There is a twist…the books must be standing up, not lying flat!

**Super Stacker:** _____ **How Many:** _____

**My Amazing World Record:** _____

## Balance Beam

Who can balance a yardstick on her finger for the longest?

**The Winner:** _____ **Time:** _____

**My Amazing World Record:** _____

Now see who can walk the farthest while doing just that!

**The Winner:** _____ **Time:** _____

**My Amazing World Record:** _____

# Bunch of Fruit

Get a bunch of grapes (at least 25). Who can hold the most in one hand? Stacking them is okay!

**The Winner:** _____ **How Many:**_____

**My Amazing World Record:** _____

# Thumbthing Fun!

Thumb wrestling is fun, and doing it with eyes shut even more so! So grab your opponent's hand, close your eyes, keep your elbows on the table the whole time, and see who wins the best of three thumb war battles!

**The Winner:** _____

# Face-to-Face

This is a challenge of balance and comedy. Stand on one foot face-to-face with your opponent, two feet apart. Now make silly faces. No touching! Whoever puts her foot down first is the loser! Who can stand that way the longest?

**The Winner:** _____

**Time:** _____

## Amazing Fact

*People worldwide do yoga to help learn balance and flexibility, which are useful in these challenges. Yoga began in India more than 5,000 years ago.*

# FUN Classwork!

The other group games were for random sets of kids. These are for an entire classroom. Ask your teacher to help organize these and see what sort of records you set together!

## Oh, Snap, Part II

How many finger snaps can your class make together in a row? They have to be completely simultaneous, which means at the exact same moment. They need to sound like one giant snap!

**First Attempt:** _____

**Our Amazing World Record:** _____

### Amazing Fact

*Imelda Marcos was the wife of the Philippines' former longtime leader, Ferdinand Marcos. She collected more than 3,000 shoes in her closet by the time the Marcoses were kicked out of office.*

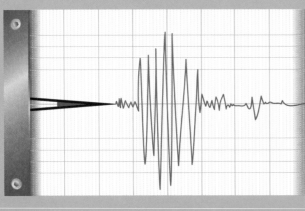

## Earthquake!

How many times can you all jump together? Everyone has to be off the ground at once! Your teacher should keep watch and count.

**First Attempt:** _____

**Our Amazing World Record:** _____

# Class Togetherness

See how long you can go at recess with your entire class holding hands. No matter where you go and no matter whose nose itches, hold on! Time yourself and see if you can improve day to day!

**First Attempt:** _____

**Our Amazing World Record:** _____

# Shoe Scramble

Put all your shoes into a large box. Put the box 25 yards away. Then race to see how long it takes all the kids in your class to get all their shoes back on and race back to the start. All laces must be tied!

**First Attempt:** _____

**Our Amazing World Record:** _____

# Talk-a-thon

Line up and see how fast your entire class can say the alphabet with each person saying one letter at a time. Then see how high you can count—one at a time—in one minute.

**Alphabet:** _____

**Counting:** _____

**Our Amazing World Record:** _____

**Our Amazing World Record:** _____

# Working Together

Three's a crowd, but two's a team! Get your best pal and set a stack of personal world records together. How many times can you do each of these activities? Not all at once, though that would be fun to try, too!

## How Many Times can You.....

| | First Attempt | Our Amazing World Record |
|---|---|---|

**Toss a water balloon back and forth without dropping it?**
From 6 feet away
From 10 feet away
From 20 feet away

**Toss a raw egg back and forth? Game is over when it breaks!**
From 4 feet away
From 8 feet away
From 12 feet away

**Throw a Frisbee back and forth (catching it each time)?**
From 20 feet away
From 30 feet away
From 40 feet away

**Kick a ball back and forth without missing? One kick each time!**
From 10 feet away
From 20 feet away
From 30 feet away

# Friends in Disguise!

For this one, you need a blindfold and several friends. Put the blindfold on and then see how well you do at guessing who each person is. The first time, you can only touch their face before guessing. The second time, just touch their hair. The third time, they can talk...but they should disguise their voices.

**First Attempt:** _____

**Our Amazing**
**World Record:** _____

| | First Attempt | Our Amazing World Record |
|---|---|---|
| Volley a ball over a net? The ball can't hit the ground. | _____ | _____ |
| Jump rope—both of you sharing one jump rope? | _____ | _____ |
| Jump rope backward (still sharing the same rope)? | _____ | _____ |
| Jump rope with each of you facing opposite directions? (Yes, still with the same rope!) | _____ | _____ |

# Balance... and Beam!

## Hand Walker

Get help from a friend. Have her hold your legs while you do a handstand. Then see how far you can "walk" before your arms get too tired to continue.

**First Attempt:** _____

**My Amazing
World Record:** _____

**Super Challenge:** How far can you handstand-walk *without* your friend holding your legs?

**First Attempt:** _____

**My Amazing
World Record:** _____

### Amazing Fact

*The woman with the most Olympic gymnastics medals is Larisa Latynina of the Soviet Union. She earned her total—the most by a woman in any sport—from 1956 to 1964. She brought home 18 medals: nine gold, five silver, and four bronze.*

## Balance Curb

Find a long, low curb and make like a gymnast. How far can you walk this narrow balance beam without toppling?

**First Attempt:** _____

**My Amazing
World Record:** _____

For more of a challenge, mark out a distance and see how fast you can walk it.

# Hoop Dive

Have a friend hold a Hula-Hoop so that it is straight up and down about a foot above the ground. How many times can you jump back and forth through it in a minute?

**First Attempt:** _____

**My Amazing
World Record:** _____

**Super Challenge:** Now have her hold the hoop two or three feet off the ground!

**First Attempt:** _____

**My Amazing
World Record:** _____

# Be a Tree!*

Stand up straight and lift one foot and place it just above your other leg's knee. How long can you stay balanced in this position before you have to put your foot down?

**First Attempt:** _____

**My Amazing
World Record:** _____

# Vault to Victory

In gymnastics, athletes leap over the vaulting horse. In this challenge, you and a friend hop over each other. See how fast you can take turns hopping over each other to cover 20 yards. Challenge tip: Crouch down low to make the hopping easier!

**First Attempt:** _____

**My Amazing
World Record:** _____

# GO FOR THE GOLD

In the Summer Olympics, track and field is one of the most popular categories of competition. "Track" simply means the running events. "Field" is all the other stuff: jumping, throwing, and vaulting! See how you do at these Olympic-like challenges.

## The Flying Sock!

Instead of the hammer throw, it's the sock toss! Pack your biggest sock with five other socks. Twirl and fling! How far can you launch it? (Too far for your measuring tape? See page 7 for how to make a measuring string.)

**First Attempt:** _____

**My Amazing World Record:** _____

## One Giant Leap

Olympic long jumpers get a running start. In this one, you don't! Put your feet together and jump as far as you can. Measure from where your heels land. How far did you jump?

**First Attempt:** _____

**My Amazing World Record:** _____

# The 25-Yard Hsad!*

*That's "dash" backward...and that's what you have to do. How fast can you run 25 yards...backward?

**First Attempt:** _____

**My Amazing World Record:** _____

# Ready, Aim...Spear!

Olympic athletes throw the spear-like javelin. For this challenge, cut out a piece of paper into a one-foot circle. Put it on the ground. Now take a straight stick about three feet long and see if you can throw it like a javelin to hit the target from 10 feet away...then back up. From how far away can you throw it on target?

**First Attempt:** _____

**My Amazing World Record:** _____

# How Low Will You Go?

Instead of the high jump, we'll do the low crawl. Have friends hold a stick or pole. Crawl under it. How low can the bar be to the ground before you can't make it under?

**First Attempt:** _____

**My Amazing World Record:** _____

## Amazing Fact

*American Betty Robinson won the first Olympic track medal for women. The 16-year-old won the 100-meter dash in 1928.*

# pool power!

*Splish, splash,* it's time to set some records. Head to the pool with a parent and try your best at these watery challenges. For many of these, it would be helpful to have a parent or friend keeping time!

## Wet Wardrobe

Grab a T-shirt, shorts, and a pair of socks and throw them into the shallow end of the pool. Now get in the pool and start timing. How long does it take to get dressed and out of the pool?

**First Attempt:** _____

**My Amazing World Record:** _____

**Super Challenge:** Add a sweatshirt and sweatpants to your wet wardrobe!

**First Attempt:** _____

**My Amazing World Record:** _____

## Splash Sprint

How fast can you get across the pool? No, wait…not swimming. You have to run! Do the race in the part of the pool in which the water is waist to chest high.

**First Attempt:** _____

**My Amazing World Record:** _____

**Extra Challenge:** At the shallow end, see how fast you can cross the pool by walking on your knees!

# Dive for Five (Cents)

Have a friend or parent drop five pennies into the pool. How quickly can you get them all out of the water? You can remove only one at a time.

**First Attempt:** _____

**My Amazing
World Record:** _____

# Try It with Friends!

Toss five pennies, quarters, nickels, and dimes into the pool. After three minutes, stop the game and add up everyone's change. Who collected the most money?

**Richest Friend:** _____

**My Grand Total:** _____

# Pool Ball

How fast can you get a balloon across the pool without touching it? Time to use your imagination!

**First Attempt:** _____

**My Amazing
World Record:** _____

Try the same thing with a Ping-Pong ball!

**First Attempt:** _____

**My Amazing
World Record:** _____

# Not a Drop!

Put on an old baseball cap. How fast can you swim (not walk) back and forth across the pool four times while keeping that hat completely dry? Watch out for splashes!

**First Attempt:** _____

**My Amazing
World Record:** _____

# Awesome Animals

**Check out these tough but fuzzy, furry, and feathery challenges from the animal world.**

## Bird Brain

How many different types of birds can you name in 30 seconds? No repeats!

**First Attempt:** _____

**My Amazing World Record:** _____

Do well at that? Then let's see how well you know some other animal groupings. Same rules: Name as many as you can in 30 seconds!

| | First Attempt | My Amazing World Record |
|---|---|---|
| Dog breeds | _____ | _____ |
| Ocean fish | _____ | _____ |
| Dinosaurs | _____ | _____ |
| Insects | _____ | _____ |
| Animals that live in the cold | _____ | _____ |
| Animals that live in the heat | _____ | _____ |
| Animals found at a pet store | _____ | _____ |
| Animals that make people go "ewwww!" | _____ | _____ |

# Animal Relay

Run four 20-yard laps, each in the style of one of these four creatures: monkey, penguin, kangaroo, snake. What's your best time? (Hint: Snakes move better on grass!)

**First Attempt:** _____

**My Amazing World Record:** _____

# Super-Duper Zooper

You'll need a friend for this one. Have her read this list of animal babies to you and see how many adults you can match to them in 15 seconds.

| Baby names | Adult animals | First Attempt | My Amazing World Record |
|---|---|---|---|
| Puppy | Dog | ☐ | ☐ |
| Kitten | Cat | ☐ | ☐ |
| Calf | Cow | ☐ | ☐ |
| Cub | Bear | ☐ | ☐ |
| Fledgling | Eagle or Hawk | ☐ | ☐ |
| Fawn | Deer | ☐ | ☐ |
| Tadpole | Frog | ☐ | ☐ |
| Kid | Goat | ☐ | ☐ |
| Foal | Horse | ☐ | ☐ |
| Joey | Kangaroo | ☐ | ☐ |
| Owlet | Owl | ☐ | ☐ |
| Cygnet | Swan | ☐ | ☐ |

# Flower Power

They bring color to our world and brightness to our homes. Here are some fun challenges that show your love and knowledge of the floral world.

## Forget Me Not!

Here's an easy place to start. How many flower types can you name in 30 seconds?

**First Attempt:** _____

**My Amazing World Record:** _____

## Color Me Red

How fast can you name one type of flower that is found in the following colors? Have someone read you the color, record your answer so you can check later, and also keep time.

| Color: | Flower: | Time: |
|---|---|---|
| **Purple** | _____ | _____ |
| **Red** | _____ | _____ |
| **Orange** | _____ | _____ |
| **Gold** | _____ | _____ |
| **Yellow** | _____ | _____ |
| **White** | _____ | _____ |
| **Pink** | _____ | _____ |

## Amazing Fact

*The 2013 All-America Rose was the Francis Meilland Hybrid Tea Rose. New roses are bred each year and one is named the nation's best!*

# Secret Scent

For this challenge you'll need a blindfold and a place with several types of flowers. Put on the blindfold and with a friend holding the flowers or leading you to them, see how many different types of flowers you can name just from their smell.

**First Attempt:** _____

**My Amazing
World Record:** _____

# What a Wig!*

You have to pick dandelions to weed the grass anyway. Let's make it fun! In one minute, how many can you pick AND stick into your hair? Take turns seeing who can make the wildest flower wig!

**First Attempt:** _____

**My Amazing
World Record:** _____

# Winners Announced in Spring

This is a long-term challenge. Get several friends and buy some flower seeds. Each of you take five seeds and plant them. Over the next few weeks, help them grow with water, food, and light. After each month, measure and see who is growing the tallest plants! Add up the heights from all five for your total.

**First Attempt:** _____

**My Amazing
World Record:** _____

# SNOW PROBLEM!

These challenges demand some winter weather. Grab your hat, coat, boots, and mittens and head out into the cold!

## Super Swoosh!

Head for the hills with your sled or snow tube! Always start from the same place. What is the longest ride you can take down the hill without stopping?

**Amazing Fact**

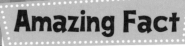

In 1911, the town of Tamarack, California, had the deepest snowfall ever recorded. The massive drifts measured 37.7 feet deep!

**First Attempt:** _____

**My Amazing World Record:** _____

Race a friend or two! Set up a finish line at the bottom of the hill. Who wins the most sled races out of 10?

**First Attempt:** _____

**My Amazing World Record:** _____

## Amazing Angels

You need a nice field of snow for this one (and gloves and a hat, probably!). In 30 seconds, how many complete snow angels can you make?

**First Attempt:** _____

**My Amazing World Record:** _____

## Ice Darts

Find some icicles and make a circular target on your lawn (about two feet across). Stand at least 30 feet away. How many bull's-eyes can you get out of five icicle throws?

**First Attempt:** _____

**My Amazing World Record:** _____

# Make a Pet

Snowmen are simple to make. But how about snow animals? Have a contest with friends: Who can create the best snow sculpture of an animal in 30 minutes! Think snakes, turtles, penguins, frogs, and other animals with easy-to-recognize shapes.

**First Attempt:** _____

**My Amazing World Record:** _____

# Slog Races

Running through snow can be tougher than running through water! But it sure is fun. See how fast you can run across a snowy yard or field. Better yet, challenge friends or family members to a race!

**First Attempt:** _____

**My Amazing World Record:** _____

# Snow Mountain

Grab a bucket, shovel, or whatever tools you wish. The challenge: Build the tallest snow pile you can in five minutes. Can you make a pile that's taller than you?

**First Attempt:** _____

**My Amazing World Record:** _____

**Super Challenge:** What's the biggest snowball you can make? Make it however you wish: rolling, packing, shoveling. The only rule is that you need to be able to pick it up and hold it for at least five seconds!

**First Attempt:** _____

**My Amazing World Record:** _____

# Into the Wild!

The world of nature will be the arena for these challenges. Alone or with friends, these tasks will lead you away from civilization, into the heart of the great outdoors, far from humans, light, and comfort! At least until dinnertime, that is. Bring a stopwatch and a handy bag for collecting.

## Team Tracker

For this challenge, you'll need several friends and a blindfold. Find a level, safe area of woods, trees, or brush. The first two "trackers" move about 25 yards away from the others. Then it's a race to see how fast they can return to the other group. Here's the challenge: One person is blindfolded and the other person must use words only to guide her partner back to the group. No touching! Then swap places and see if you can beat the first time.

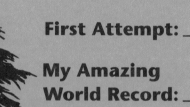

**First Attempt:** _____

**My Amazing
World Record:** _____

## Silent Sneaker

Have a friend sit facing away from you in an outdoor area, such as the woods or a field. Move about 20 feet away from her. Have her close her eyes. Now…can you tag her without her hearing you? You'll have to move slowly and oh-so-silently, like a tiger stalking prey!

**First Attempt:** _____

**My Amazing
World Record:** _____

# Minute Madness!

In one-minute races, see who can find:

| | Team A | Team B |
|---|---|---|
| The most types of tree leaves | _____ | _____ |
| The most colors of rocks | _____ | _____ |
| Something you can eat | _____ | _____ |
| The coolest living insect | _____ | _____ |
| Evidence of another animal<br>*(wings, fur, hair, tracks, etc.)* | _____ | _____ |
| Sticks that look like letters | _____ | _____ |
| The prettiest flower<br>*(don't pick it, though; let it keep growing!)* | _____ | _____ |
| An animal home<br>*(beehive, squirrel den, bird's nest, or even an ant hill)* | _____ | |

# Sand Race

You might need a beach or a big sandbox for this one: Set up a distance for a foot race, perhaps about 25 yards. Now—race! Oh, wait, we forgot to mention that your feet can't leave the sand…you have to shuffle as fast as you can!

**First Attempt:** _____

**My Amazing
World Record:** _____

# Kitchen Klassics!

Time to have fun in the kitchen…and we don't mean doing dishes! Check with your folks before you start rummaging around the kitchen. Then see how you do with these challenges.

## Food Smarts

We'll start with some easy timed challenges that don't require any gear at all, other than a stopwatch and, if you wish, paper and pencil. How fast can you come up with the following? Work from memory, but if you get stuck, you've got the kitchen to explore!

| | First Attempt | My Amazing World Record |
|---|---|---|
| Ten types of fruit | _____ | _____ |
| Eight types of vegetables | _____ | _____ |
| Five types of noodles | _____ | _____ |
| Five types of cakes | _____ | _____ |
| Eight types of restaurants | _____ | _____ |
| Ten types of candy | _____ | _____ |
| Six dinner dishes that include meat | _____ | _____ |
| Seven types of sandwiches | _____ | _____ |
| Six types of soup | _____ | _____ |
| Twelve yummy toppings for a pizza | _____ | _____ |
| Six foods that are packaged in bags | _____ | _____ |

# An A-Peel-ing Challenge

What's the longest unbroken apple peel you can make? Be careful, as peelers are sharp. If you haven't peeled an apple before, ask a parent to show you the technique. Best part about this challenge? Every time you try, you get an apple to eat!

**First Attempt:** _____

**My Amazing World Record:** _____

## Amazing Fact

*A man named David Goodell made nineteenth-century housewives very happy. In 1864, he invented the first popular apple-peeling device.*

# Get the Point?

Take all the spoons you have in the house and put them in a small box (a shoe box works well). Then have someone add one fork to the box. While blindfolded, how long does it take you to find the fork?

**First Attempt:** _____

**My Amazing World Record:** _____

# Beans, Baby!

Get a half-pound of dry red beans and a half-pound of dry white beans. Mix them together in a bowl. Now…wash your hands! Then see how fast you can sort them back into their own colors!

**First Attempt:** _____

**My Amazing World Record:** _____

# COOL AT SCHOOL

Those games you play at recess are about to get intense! Test your skills while setting new world records with these familiar objects.

## Hoop It Up!

Hula-Hoops are not only incredibly fun, but also wonderful exercise. So get hooping! Start with the basic challenge: How long can you keep a Hula-Hoop spinning around your waist?

**First Attempt:** _____

**My Amazing World Record:** _____

Getting good at hooping? See how long you can keep two hoops spinning at the same time!

**First Attempt:** _____

**My Amazing World Record:** _____

**Bonus Challenge:** Transform your hoop into a jump rope! How many times can you jump through the hoop before missing?

**First Attempt:** _____

**My Amazing World Record:** _____

## Four-Square Forever

You need three friends for this one. Play Four-Square, but try not to get the other players out. How many hits can you make without a miss?

**First Attempt:** _____

**My Amazing World Record:** _____

1  2
4  3

# Serious Hopscotch

Sure, hopscotch is fun, but now…
it's serious! What's your fastest
speed for hopping up and back
through the entire hopscotch
layout? Don't touch the lines!

**First Attempt:** _____

**My Amazing
World Record:** _____

# Bunny Ball Hop

Put a kickball ball between your feet. Now see how far
you can hop without losing the ball.

**First Attempt:** _____

**My Amazing
World Record:** _____

Now try it with a tennis ball! Think
that's easy? Add another tennis ball!

**First Attempt:** _____

**My Amazing
World Record:** _____

# Arts Smarts

Be a great artist...using not only your hands, but also your feet or mouth! These challenges test your unique artistic skills!

## Chalk Line Challenge

What is the longest line you can make outside with one piece of chalk? You can't take the chalk off the ground once you start.

**First Attempt:** _____

**My Amazing World Record:** _____

## Foot Writing

How many three-letter words can you write holding a pen or pencil between your toes? See how many you can do in three minutes.

**First Attempt:** _____

**My Amazing World Record:** _____

## Toothy Talent

Use a paintbrush or markers to create a rainbow. Easy, right? You have to do it holding the brush or marker in your teeth! How quickly can you paint the rainbow?

**First Attempt:** _____

**My Amazing World Record:** _____

## Amazing Fact

*In 2013, a three-panel painting was sold for a new all-time record. The work by Francis Bacon (yes...his real name!) sold for $142 million! Might make you pay more attention in art class, huh?*

# Super-Duper Challenge: Foot Feats

How talented are your feet? Writing is just one of the odd ways you can use your feet. We've thought of others. Practice these other fantastic foot feats and record the dates of your success:

| | Date of My First Attempt | Date I Mastered the Skill |
|---|---|---|
| Hold a spoon. Can you feed yourself? That's cool, but GROSS! | _____ | _____ |
| Brush your hair— or your pet's hair! | _____ | _____ |
| Pick up pencils from the floor. Can you pick up two at a time? | _____ | _____ |
| Throw a small ball. Remember to record your distances! | _____ | _____ |
| Play "Mary Had a Little Lamb" on a piano. | _____ | _____ |
| Paint a picture. | _____ | _____ |
| Use a calculator to do some math problems. | _____ | _____ |
| Use the remote control to turn on your TV and find your favorite channel. | _____ | _____ |

# RUBBER and String

You'll need rubber bands and a ball of string or twine for these challenges. Most also need a pair of scissors. Always ask a parent before borrowing or using objects from around the house!

## Clip and Spell

How fast can you cut short pieces of string and form them into the letters AMAZING ME?

**First Attempt:** _____

**My Amazing
World Record:** _____

Now take those same pieces of string and use them all to make your name. You have to use all the pieces!

**First Attempt:** _____

**My Amazing
World Record:** _____

## Set a Record? Knot!

How many knots can you tie in two feet of string? They must be next to each other so they can be counted!

**First Attempt:** _____

**My Amazing
World Record:** _____

## Hide the Lead!

Take a pencil that's at least six inches long. How fast can you wrap it in string so that you can't see any part of the pencil (including the ends)?

**First Attempt:** _____

**My Amazing
World Record:** _____

# A Hand and a Band

How far can you shoot a rubber band using your hand? Try different band sizes to get the maximum distance!

**First Attempt:** _____

**My Amazing
World Record:** _____

# Super Challenge: Rubber (Band) Ball

This challenge could take a very long time. Collect all the rubber bands you can find and make a rubber-band ball. How big can you make it? Record your progress here:

_____

_____

_____

_____

_____

How high can your rubber-band ball bounce?

**First Attempt:** _____

**My Amazing
World Record:** _____

## Amazing Fact

*A man named Joel Waul created the world's largest rubber-band ball. It weighed 9,032 pounds and stood almost seven feet tall.*

# Trivia Time!

**?** **?** **?**

So you think you know a lot of stuff, do you? Well, it's time to put that mighty brain to the test. Start thinking!

## Animal Alphabet

How fast can you write an alphabetical list of animals from "A" to "Z"? Try it again without repeating any of the animals from the first list!

**First Attempt:** _____

**My Amazing
World Record:** _____

## Crazy for Countries

Repeat this challenge, but use the names of countries instead!

**First Attempt:** _____

**My Amazing
World Record:** _____

### Amazing Fact

*If you're counting countries and you get to 200, you went too far. According to the U.S. government, there are 195 countries in the world (as of 2013).*

# List Crazy!

How many items in each of these categories can you say (with no repeats!) in one minute? You will need someone keeping count for you as you speak. You can also make these head-to-head challenges with your friends by writing your answers instead of saying them.

| | First Attempt | My Amazing World Record |
|---|---|---|
| Names of your friends | _____ | _____ |
| Countries of the world | _____ | _____ |
| Words that start with "Q" | _____ | _____ |
| Words that start with "Z" | _____ | _____ |
| Types of dogs | _____ | _____ |
| Names of candy bars | _____ | _____ |
| Things that live underground | _____ | _____ |
| Names of flowers | _____ | _____ |
| Cartoon characters | _____ | _____ |
| Things you find in a classroom | _____ | _____ |
| Famous people in music | _____ | _____ |
| Books you have read (start with this one!) | _____ | _____ |
| Noises animals make | _____ | _____ |
| Things in the sky or in space | _____ | _____ |
| Famous buildings | _____ | _____ |
| Onomatopoeia* words | _____ | _____ |
| World languages | _____ | _____ |
| Types of music | _____ | _____ |
| Types of musical instruments | _____ | _____ |

*Great word, huh? It means the use of words that stand for sounds: "bang," "zip," "pow," "hiss," etc.

# michelangelo Who?

Do you have what it takes to be a great sculptor? Maybe. But these challenges are all about setting records, not creating art!

## Potato Pyramid

Next time you have mashed potatoes for dinner, try this! How fast can you make a potato pyramid that's at least three inches tall? Don't forget to eat your work when you're done!

**First Attempt:** _____

**My Amazing
World Record:** _____

## Dribble It

You will need a beach or sandbox for this one. What is the tallest drip castle you can build? To make one, take very wet sand in your fist, squeeze, and let it dribble out the bottom. Keep dribbling on the same spot to build your spire!

**First Attempt:** _____

**My Amazing
World Record:** _____

## Heavy Metal?

How quickly can you make a spider out of tin foil? It must have eight legs and stand tall enough so the body isn't touching the table.

**First Attempt:** _____

**My Amazing
World Record:** _____

# Super Challenge: Dough Play

Play-Doh is not just for little kids! It's great for setting world records! Each of these challenges needs exactly one can of Play-Doh! For each, you MUST use the whole can.

Make the longest snake you can. Your snake may be as thin as you want, but must not have any breaks!

**First Attempt:** _____

**My Amazing World Record:** _____

How many perfect snowmen can you make? Each must have three balls of different sizes and must stand on its own. They can be as big or small as you want.

**First Attempt:** _____

**My Amazing World Record:** _____

How many pretzels can you make?

**First Attempt:** _____

**My Amazing World Record:** _____

How quickly can you form the entire alphabet? Use capital letters to make it easier.

**First Attempt:** _____

**My Amazing World Record:** _____

Capitals too easy for you? Try sculpting all lowercase letters. What was your time?

**First Attempt:** _____

**My Amazing World Record:** _____

## Amazing Fact

*Mount Rushmore in South Dakota is one of the world's most famous sculptures. The creator, Gutzon Borglum, needed 14 years to complete the four-president masterpiece.*

# Mall Mania!

C'mon, who doesn't love to shop? Even if you're not buying anything, just looking around is fun. For these challenges, you'll need an adult to let you loose in some stores. Actual purchasing is optional; having fun is not!

## Color Matching

Challenge a friend to see who can find one piece of clothing with a main color that is one of the colors of the rainbow. Whoever gets all seven first wins!

**First Attempt:** _____

**My Amazing World Record:** _____

## Mallphabet

In a mall or a place with numerous stores, try to find one thing for sale that starts with each letter of the alphabet. Bring a notebook or snap pix with your phone to keep track! How fast can you find all the letters?

**First Attempt:** _____

**My Amazing World Record:** _____

## Amazing Fact

The world's largest department store might be worth a trip to Busan, South Korea. The Shinsegae ("New World") Centum City department store has more than three million square feet of shopping. That's as big as 50 football fields put together!

## Silent Shopping

How good are you at mime? Can you enter a store, "ask" for help finding something, describe it, and buy it… all without saying a word?

**First Attempt:** _____

**My Amazing
World Record:** _____

## Bargain Hunter

Team up with some friends for an attack on a mall. In 15 minutes, who can come back with the biggest bargain: That is, the item of clothing that was marked down the most, either in dollars or by percent.

**First Attempt:** _____

**My Amazing
World Record:** _____

## Thrift-y Shopping

With an imaginary five dollars in hand at a thrift store, how fast can you pull together a complete outfit of shirt, pants, and accessory? Don't worry about how it would look—just about how much it costs!

**First Attempt:** _____

**My Amazing
World Record:** _____

# FABULOUS FOOD!

The coolest part about these challenges? You get to eat whatever you use to set the records!

## One-Handed Chef

How fast can you make a peanut-butter-and-jelly sandwich on two pieces of bread... using only one hand? That includes opening the jars, spreading the stuff, cutting the bread...and cleaning up! For a bonus, try doing it with your "opposite" hand.

**First Attempt:** _____

**My Amazing World Record:** _____

## Pudding Plaster

Make some pudding; chocolate looks best for this, but pick your favorite flavor. Put about two cups on a plate. Then have a race to see who can move the pudding from the plate into a smaller bowl. Seems easy, right? Oh, wait...you can only use your mouth. No hands, not even on the plate! Slurp up the pudding and spit it back out into the other bowl. Yes, it's pretty gross, but that's part of the fun! If you don't want to race, then go for the best time.

**First Attempt:** _____

**My Amazing World Record:** _____

# Yo-Yo Yogurt

Get a small container of your favorite yogurt. How fast can you eat it? Put that spoon down, though: For this challenge you have to use a fork!

**First Attempt:** _____

**My Amazing
World Record:** _____

## Amazing Fact

*Next time you eat peanut butter, think of African-American scientist George Washington Carver. In the late 1800s, he not only found a better way to make the tasty stuff, but came up with over 300 uses for peanuts.*

# How Do You Spell "Raisin"?

For this challenge, you need a good-sized box of raisins. Pick up a magazine and randomly point to a word. Then see who can spell the word fastest using only raisins to form the letters on the counter.

**First Attempt:** _____

**My Amazing
World Record:** _____

# Keep 'em Separated

Get one cup each of peanuts, raisins, M&M's, and a Cheerios-like cereal. Mix all four cups together into one larger bowl. Time yourself to see how fast you can split the four foods back into their cups. No fair eating some to make it go faster!

**First Attempt:** _____

**My Amazing
World Record:** _____

# FAST FASHION

Are you ready to hit the runway and star in the fashion world? Before you get your face in famous magazines, you have to face our challenges! Test your knowledge with the categories on the opposite page. Plus…

## Dress in the Dark

You'll need a big closet and lots of friends for this challenge. Take turns putting on a blindfold and trying to put together a complete outfit from clothes scattered all around you. At the end, vote for the winners for "best dressed," "craziest costume," and "color-blind…really!"

**Best Dressed:** _____

**Craziest Costume:** _____

**Color-Blind:** _____

## Shirt Tales

Go into your father's or brother's closet (with their permission, of course) and assemble and put on the most cool, in-style outfit you can in just one minute. See what your family or friends think!

**First Attempt:** _____

**My Amazing World Record:** _____

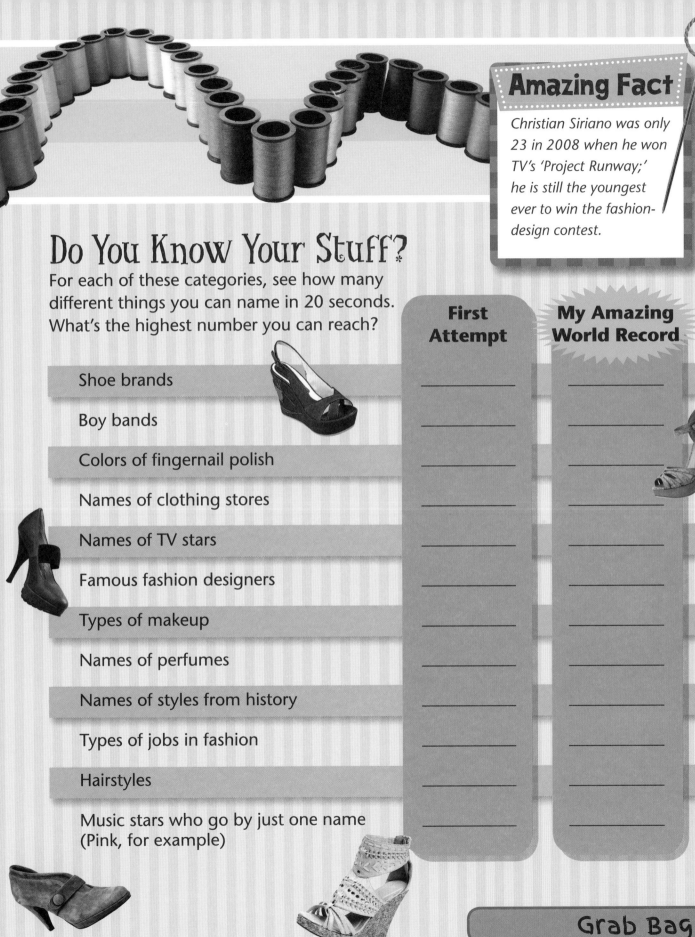

**Amazing Fact**

Christian Siriano was only 23 in 2008 when he won TV's 'Project Runway;' he is still the youngest ever to win the fashion-design contest.

# Do You Know Your Stuff?

For each of these categories, see how many different things you can name in 20 seconds. What's the highest number you can reach?

| | First Attempt | My Amazing World Record |
|---|---|---|
| Shoe brands | _____ | _____ |
| Boy bands | _____ | _____ |
| Colors of fingernail polish | _____ | _____ |
| Names of clothing stores | _____ | _____ |
| Names of TV stars | _____ | _____ |
| Famous fashion designers | _____ | _____ |
| Types of makeup | _____ | _____ |
| Names of perfumes | _____ | _____ |
| Names of styles from history | _____ | _____ |
| Types of jobs in fashion | _____ | _____ |
| Hairstyles | _____ | _____ |
| Music stars who go by just one name (Pink, for example) | _____ | _____ |

# And Don't Forget...

We just didn't know where else to put these challenges, but we didn't want you to miss the chance to try them.

## Rainbow Rush

In your home or your classroom, find one object for each color: red, orange, yellow, green, blue, and purple. How fast can you find the rainbow?

**First Attempt:** _____

**My Amazing World Record:** _____

## Personal Puzzle

Print out a picture of your face on a piece of copy paper. Then tear it into at least 24 pieces. How fast can you solve the jigsaw puzzle and put yourself back together?

**First Attempt:** _____

**My Amazing World Record:** _____

## Dice & Steady

Grab a Popsicle stick and five dice. Hold the Popsicle stick in your teeth. Carefully stack the dice on the very end of the stick. How long can you hold them there before they topple?

**First Attempt:** _____

**My Amazing World Record:** _____

# Money on the Move

What's the longest time you can get a coin to spin before it's completely flat on the table?

**First Attempt:** _____

**My Amazing
World Record:** _____

# Pop Goes the Record

Time to chew for the gold! How many bubble-gum bubbles can you blow and pop in 30 seconds?

**First Attempt:** _____

**My Amazing
World Record:** _____

# Artful Architects

Put on your construction helmet and let's build! For these challenges, you'll need to make something that is really big, really tall, or really long.

## Super Straw

You'll need a box of straws—or two—for this challenge. What is the longest chain of straws you can make that you can still use to drink? No other materials allowed!

**First Attempt:** _____

**My Amazing
World Record:** _____

## Pretzel Architecture

Make the tallest tower you can with 100 mini pretzel sticks and 50 mini marshmallows. How tall is your masterpiece?

**First Attempt:** _____

**My Amazing
World Record:** _____

**Super Challenge:** Add to your masterpiece. How tall can you make your tower with 300 pretzel sticks and 150 mini marshmallows?

**First Attempt:** _____

**My Amazing
World Record:** _____

## Ace High

What is the highest house of playing cards you can build? Take your time... and don't sneeze!

**First Attempt:** _____

**My Amazing
World Record:** _____

## Colossal Cube

A cube is the shape of a die: six sides of equal size. What's the biggest solid perfect cube you can make using only Lego or similar building bricks?

**First Attempt:** _____

**My Amazing
World Record:** _____

## Rubber Rope!

Love making things out of rubber bands? Try for the longest rubber band rope you can make! Knot them together as shown. (need illo)

**First Attempt:** _____

**My Amazing
World Record:** _____

Try this with your class and see how long you can make the rope in an entire school year!

**Our Amazing World Record:** _____

# Kids Rule!

Adults might be bigger or stronger, but that doesn't mean they're better! See who can set the world record in these challenges—you or the people who used to be kids. Compete with an adult for each of these challenges!

## Who's the Better Bopper?

Each challenger gets three balloons and must keep them all in the air for as long as possible. As soon as one balloon hits the floor, time's up! Who won? How long did he or she bop?

**Best Bopper:** _____

**Time:** _____

## Finger Frenzy

Put a half cup of dry rice on a large plate for each challenger. Then see who can move all that rice into a cup the fastest. Oh, wait. Did we mention you have to pick up one grain at a time with your fingers? Small fingers rule!

**Fastest Fingers:** _____

**Time:** _____

### Amazing Fact

*More than 90 percent of the world's rice is grown and eaten in Asia! There are more than 40,000 different types of rice grown around the world.*

# Too-Big Daddy

Kids have the advantage on this one: How much of yourself can you fit in a laundry basket?

**First Attempt:** _____

**My Amazing
World Record:** _____

# Nose Ball

Get a large package of cotton balls. Count them out into even piles. Then see who can move his or her pile into a bowl across the room the fastest. No hands, though. You have to pick up each cotton ball with your nose. Just breathe in…and hold it!

**Winning Nose:** _____

**Time:** _____

# Hop to It

This challenge should make everyone hoppy! Who can jump rope on one foot the longest? If you don't have two ropes, time each other separately.

**Who Won:** _____

**Time:** _____

# Name that Tune

Sit with your parents and a radio (this is a great car game). One person tunes the radio one station at a time. As soon as you know the name or artist (or both) of the tune, yell it out. You get a half point for the artist and a half point for the name of the song. First team—kids or adults— to reach 10 points is the winner!

**Winning Team:** _____

**Time:** _____

# School Race!

Who can come up with the correct answers to these five questions first, you or one of your parents? No computers, phones, or calculators allowed! But you can consult any book in the house.

| | Kid | Parent |
|---|---|---|
| What is the capital of Brazil? | _____ | _____ |
| What is 27 x 32? | _____ | _____ |
| Who was the fifth U.S. president? | _____ | _____ |
| What is the third planet from our sun? | _____ | _____ |
| Who wrote the classic book *Moby Dick*? | _____ | _____ |

# Who Is the Most "Handy"?

For these challenges, it's kid vs. adult: One-handed. See who can do each of the following the fastest, but using your "other" hand ONLY (that is, if you're right-handed, use your left hand, and vice versa).

| | Kid | Adult |
|---|---|---|
| Put on and button a dress shirt. | _____ | _____ |
| Make a peanut butter and jelly sandwich. | _____ | _____ |
| Wash five dishes (with soap!). | _____ | _____ |
| Write the names of 10 states—legibly! | _____ | _____ |
| Put on and take off a sweater. | _____ | _____ |

## Record to Beat!

According to World Record Academy, Shemika Charles is the world limbo champ. She squeezed under a bar that was just 8.5 inches off the ground!

# What's That Creaking Sound?

Put on some bouncy music and let's limbo! Who can limbo lower, the kids or the adults? How low did you go?

**Who Limboed Lowest:** _____

**My Amazing World Record:** _____

# My Own World Records

We're not the only ones who can think up challenges. You can, too! You've seen how it works: You need something fun to do that can be measured and recorded. On this page, make a list of the challenges you and your friends make up and record the results. Have fun (and, since I'm a dad, I have to say this: be careful).

**Challenge:** _____

**Results:** _____

**Challenge:** _____

**Results:** _____

**Challenge:** _____

**Results:** _____

I'm Amazing!

**Challenge:** _____

**Results:** _____

**Challenge:** _____

**Results:** _____

Amazing ME!